SIBLING MAGIC

-Written by-
Michelle Gano

-Illustrated by-
Stefanie Geyer

Sibling Magic

Copyright © 2021 Michelle Gano

All rights reserved. No part of this publication may be reproduced, distributed, or transmitted in any form or by any means, including photocopying, recording, or other electronic or mechanical methods, without the prior written permission of the publisher, except in the case of brief quotations embodied in critical reviews and certain other noncommercial uses permitted by copyright law. For permission requests, write to the author, addressed "Attention: Permissions Coordinator," to the authors website below.

ISBN: 978-1-7359615-4-5

Names, characters, and places are products of the author's imagination.
Front cover image, illustrations, and book design by Stefanie Geyer.
Published in the United States of America.
First printing edition 2021.

Visit the authors website: www.lookbeyondtheclouds.com
To connect on social media, join Michelle's Instagram community @Michelle_Gano
To see more from the illustrator, join Stefanie's Instagram community @Stefanie_Taylor_Art

To my children –
Thank you for filling our home with the most special love and Sibling Magic.

Mommy and daddy said I would be getting a baby sister soon. I wasn't sure what it would be like, but I was excited to learn how to be the best big brother.

1

I helped daddy set up the crib in baby's room.

I helped mommy clean and fold baby's clothes.

I practiced holding my baby doll every night.
I gave her kisses, read books, sang lullabies,
and rocked her in the baby swing.

When I first met my baby sister, Sibling Magic filled my heart with the most special love.

I know she can't say I love you yet, but I can hold her close and give her kisses so she feels my love.

She can't play with my toys yet, but I can put my finger in her tiny hand and watch her hold on tight.

She can't ride in my toy truck yet, but I can push her in the stroller until she falls asleep.

She can't run with me in our backyard yet,
but I can put socks on her feet to keep her warm.

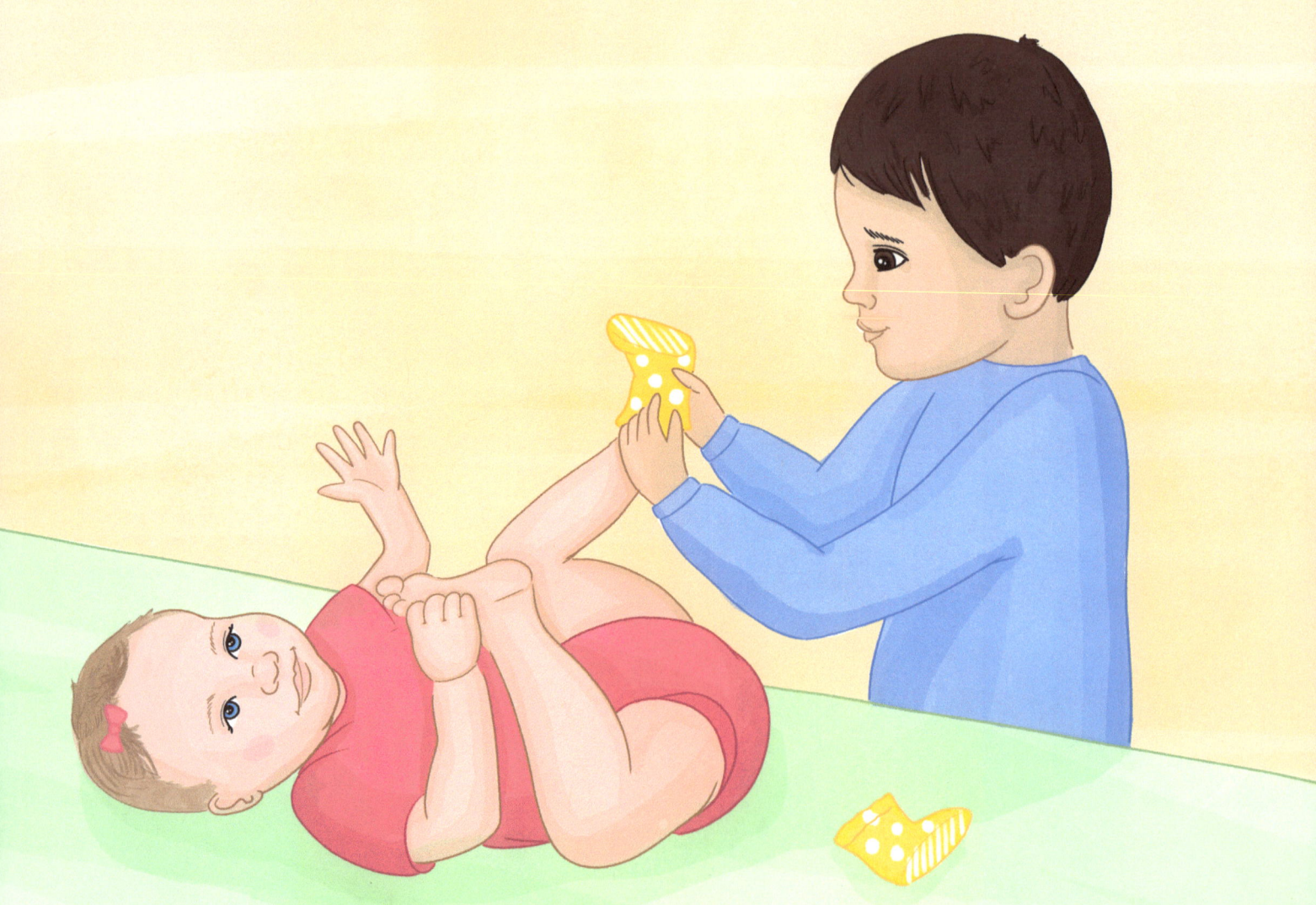

She can't eat my favorite snacks with me yet, but I can help mommy prepare her bottle.

She can't go on the potty like me yet,
but I can help daddy change her diaper.

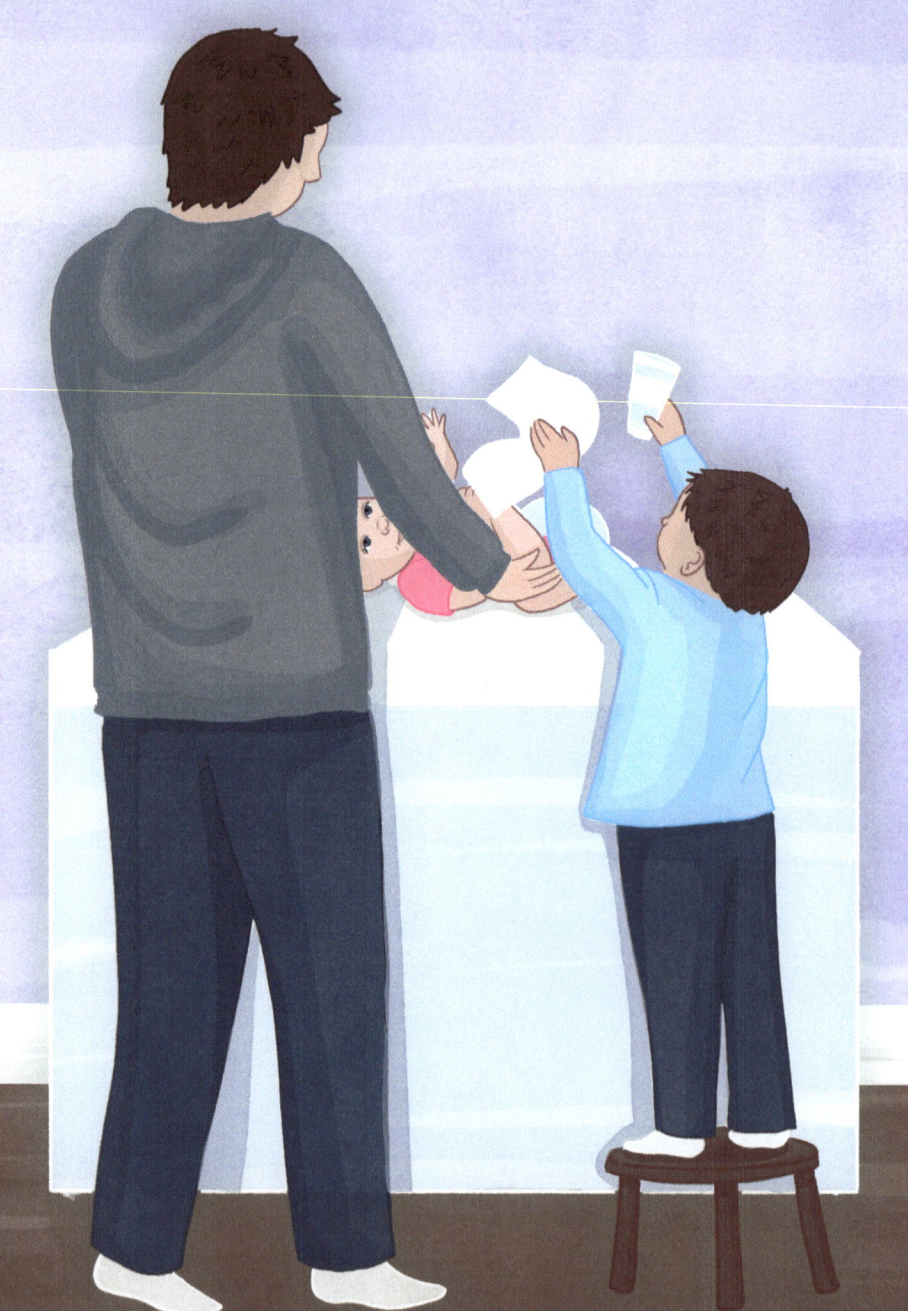

She can't splash in the bath with me yet, but I can help bathe her and wrap her in the softest towel.

She can't dance with me in the kitchen yet,
but I can sing her sweet lullabies.

She can't have tickle fights yet,
but I can make her laugh with my best silly faces.

I'm excited for the day she can do all of these things with me, but for now I'll look into her eyes and tell her she is safe and loved like mommy and daddy do for me.

"I love you."

I'll whisper in her ear as I hold her in my arms,
"Wherever this world leads us, whatever you become,
I will be your big brother cheering you on little one."

THINK ABOUT IT
- What are you excited to do with your baby brother or sister as you both grow up?
- What can you do to help baby feel loved?

NOW IT'S YOUR TURN
- Ask your parents how you can help take care of baby
- Spread Sibling Magic today by being gentle with baby, giving kisses, and making baby smile

YOUR FREE GIFT

If you love coloring as much as I do, download your own Sibling Magic coloring pages at www.lookbeyondtheclouds.com/resources

ABOUT THE AUTHOR

Michelle Gano has a special way of finding the good in each day, which inspires other people to do the same. She enjoys the simple moments in life like watching a beautiful sunrise or spending time with her husband, children, and puppy.

You can find Michelle singing and dancing around the house to Disney songs or making crafts with her family. She believes glitter makes crafts and the world a more magical place. As a mother, she appreciates the love and joy that fills her home because of her children.

Learn more about Michelle at www.lookbeyondtheclouds.com.

ABOUT THE ILLUSTRATOR

Stefanie Geyer is a children's book illustrator from Winamac, Indiana. When she's not making beautiful illustrations, you can find her enjoying nature, hiking in the woods, and gardening. She loves photography, traditional drawing, and home renovation projects.

Stefanie is an avid animal lover. She lives with Chris and their four dogs, Presley, Kimber, Roux, and Draco, and one cat, Milhouse. Her artwork inspires children to be creative and explore their own love of art.

Learn more about Stefanie on Instagram
@Stefanie_Taylor_Art

Dear Parents,

Thank you for reading this book with your children. Bringing a new baby home can be exciting and daunting all at the same time. Helping them adjust to having a little one at home can make a big difference.

One of the lessons I've learned as a mother is that your children will model your example of love. It's beautiful to witness how they love and care for other people in a similar way.

At times, their help might not feel so helpful, like when gentle kisses turn into a burst of excitement leading to a "let's push so hard that it squishes baby's face" situation or when they want to help shake the bottle and your perfectly warmed bottle spills everywhere. Always remember, they are learning how to adjust and trying their best to help just like you are.

Thank you for loving your children the way you do and for teaching them how to become compassionate individuals so our world can be a more loving place!

Love,
Michelle